I Am an Octopus
The Life of a Common Octopus

by Trisha Speed Shaskan illustrated by Todd Ouren

Special thanks to our advisers for their expertise:

Roland C. Anderson, Ph.D., Biologist
The Seattle Aquarium, Seattle, Washington

Terry Flaherty, Ph.D., Professor of English
Minnesota State University, Mankato

I Live in the Ocean

PICTURE WINDOW BOOKS
Minneapolis, Minnesota

Editor: Shelly Lyons
Designer: Lori Bye
Page Production: Melissa Kes
Art Director: Nathan Gassman
The illustrations in this book were created digitally.

Picture Window Books
151 Good Counsel Drive
P.O. Box 669
Mankato, MN 56002-0669
877-845-8392
www.picturewindowbooks.com

Printed in the United States of America.

Library of Congress Cataloging-in-Publication Data
Shaskan, Trisha Speed, 1973-
I am an octopus : the life of a common octopus /
by Trisha Speed Shaskan ; illustrated by Todd Ouren.
p. cm. — (I live in the ocean)
Includes index.
ISBN 978-1-4048-4729-3 (library binding)
1. Octopuses—Juvenile literature. I. Ouren, Todd, ill. II. Title.
QL430.3.O2S53 2008
594'.56—dc22   2008006351

I am made up of a head and a large body surrounded by eight arms. I am a common octopus. But there's nothing ordinary about me. People say I'm the smartest animal without a backbone.

Octopuses are invertebrates, or creatures without a backbone.

4

I'm a mollusk, or a soft-bodied animal. Lots of mollusks have shells, but I don't. My body is all muscle. I don't have any bones. Because of this, I can slip through cracks and small holes on the seafloor. First, my eight arms go through the cracks, and then my head.

Even a large octopus can squeeze its body through a hole the size of its own eyeball.

My body is called a mantle. It looks like a large bag. Two eyes at the top of my head give me excellent eyesight. Two gills inside my mantle help me breathe.

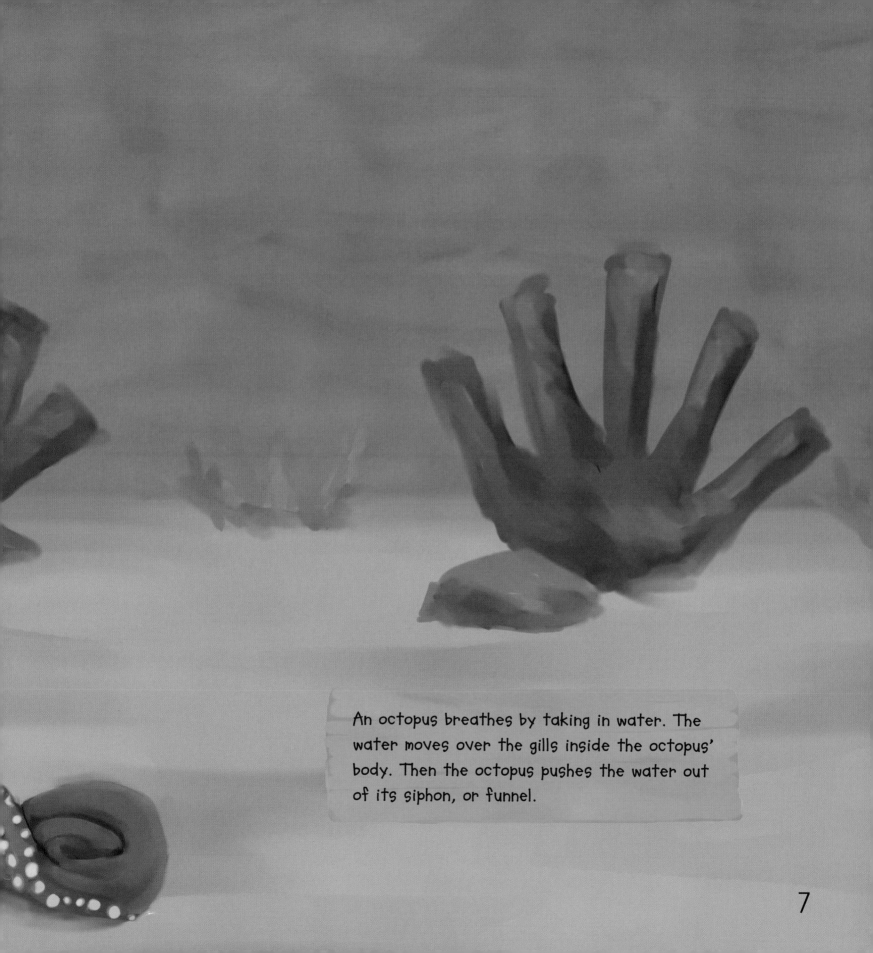

An octopus breathes by taking in water. The water moves over the gills inside the octopus' body. Then the octopus pushes the water out of its siphon, or funnel.

Sometimes I am reddish-brown. Sometimes I am orange or yellow. Can you spot me? I change the color, the pattern, and the feel of my skin to blend in and hide. It's hard for sharks to spot me.

An octopus uses special cells in its skin to change color. An octopus can look like a plant. An octopus can also make itself look like a fish. It can copy a fish's body movement, too.

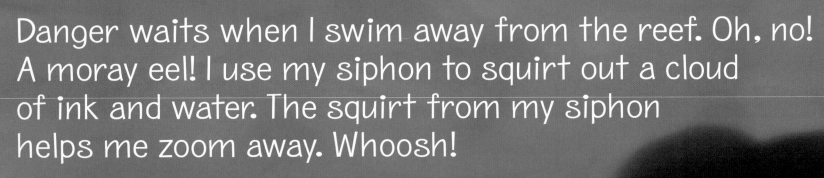

Danger waits when I swim away from the reef. Oh, no! A moray eel! I use my siphon to squirt out a cloud of ink and water. The squirt from my siphon helps me zoom away. Whoosh!

10

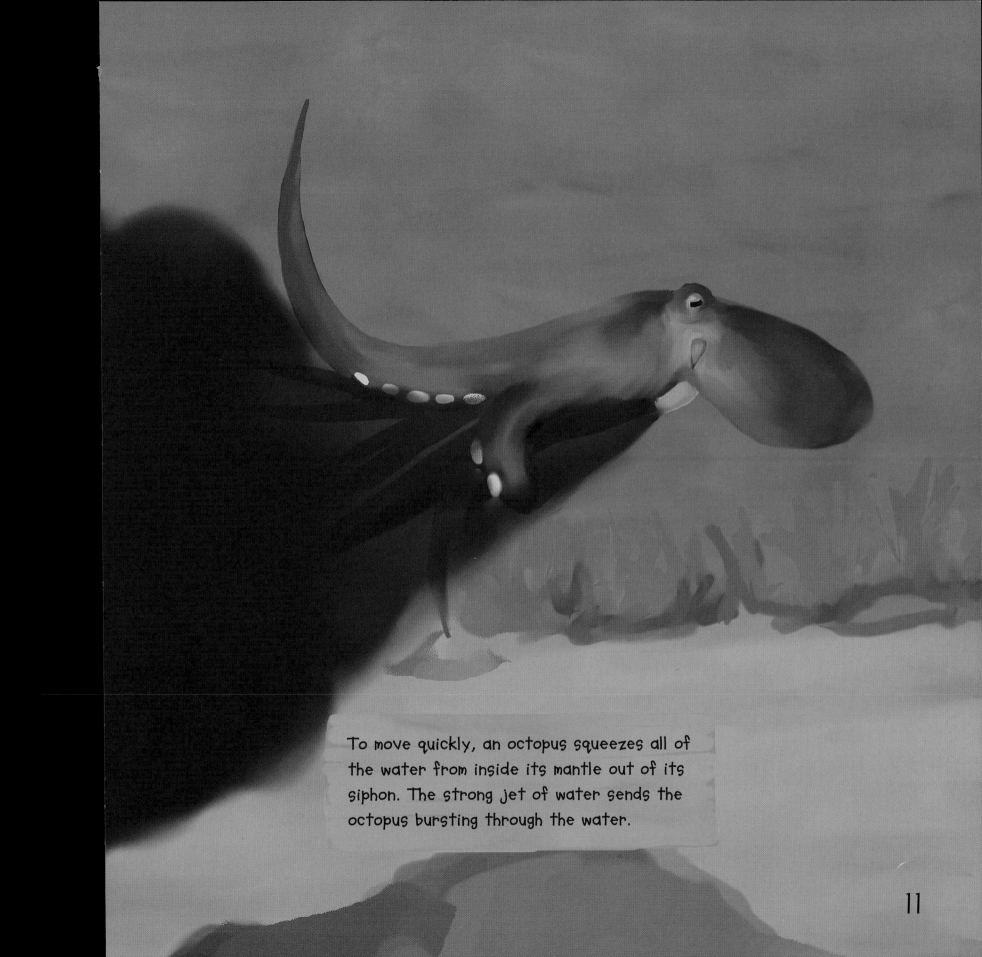

To move quickly, an octopus squeezes all of the water from inside its mantle out of its siphon. The strong jet of water sends the octopus bursting through the water.

I couldn't always protect myself. Before I was born, I was inside an egg hanging from the ceiling of my mother's den. There were thousands of eggs grouped together. Each of them was about the same color and size as a grain of rice.

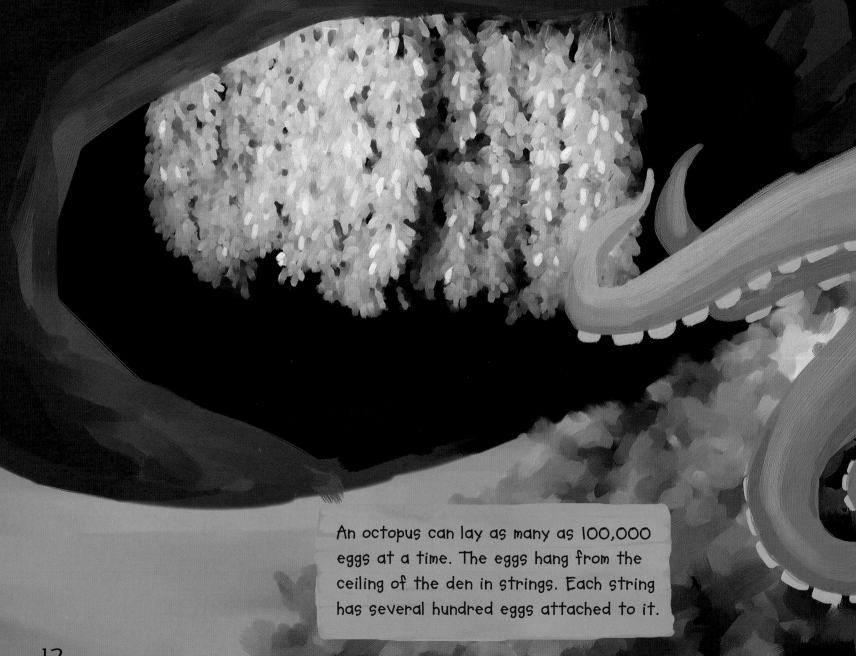

An octopus can lay as many as 100,000 eggs at a time. The eggs hang from the ceiling of the den in strings. Each string has several hundred eggs attached to it.

My mother gently pushed water out of her siphon. This washed the eggs and gave them oxygen. She also used her arms to clean the eggs. I was inside an egg for many weeks.

Then one day, I hatched. I was free to swim through the sea. But I had to move fast! Hungry fish and other animals wanted to eat me.

I drifted through the ocean for several weeks. I ate tiny animals that floated beside me.

When an octopus is born, it is only one-eighth of an inch (.32 centimeters) long. That is about the width of two quarters stacked on top of each other. A newborn octopus can change color, squirt ink, and use its siphon to move quickly.

Soon I searched along the seafloor for a den in a rock or a coral reef. I found a place inside the coral reef. That's where I live today.

You can spot an octopus' den on the ocean floor. Just look for a pile of rocks and shells. The octopus places these things there to protect itself inside the den.

At night, I move along the floor of the ocean. I stretch my arms, feeling for food inside the cracks and gaps. There's a crab! Yum!

I fan out all of my arms and cover the crab with my body. Next, I inject the crab with venom. Then, it's time to eat. I leave the crab's shell behind.

An octopus injects venom into the animals it hunts. It uses a parrot-like beak to crack the animal's shell or bones. The octopus reaches into the shell and grabs the meat with a sucker.

19

In the morning, I return to my den and drift off to sleep.

Common octopuses sleep mostly during the day.

Look Closely at a Common Octopus

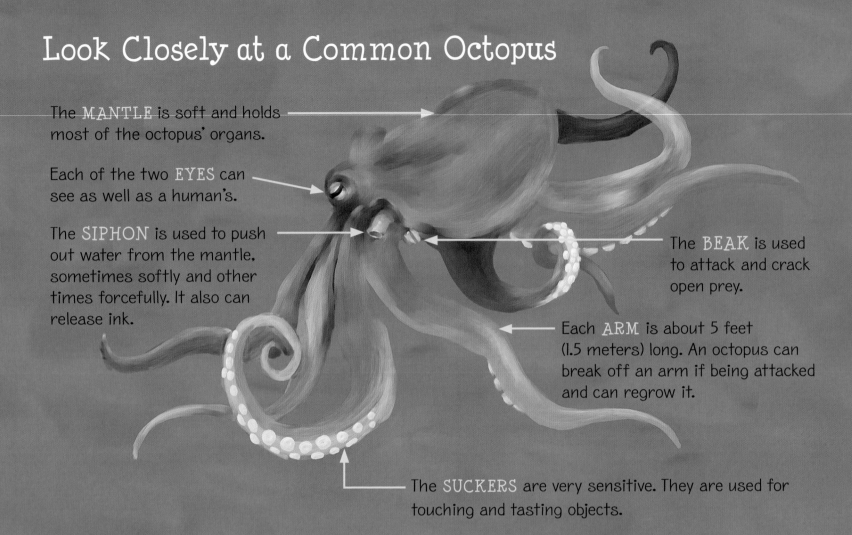

The MANTLE is soft and holds most of the octopus' organs.

Each of the two EYES can see as well as a human's.

The SIPHON is used to push out water from the mantle, sometimes softly and other times forcefully. It also can release ink.

The BEAK is used to attack and crack open prey.

Each ARM is about 5 feet (1.5 meters) long. An octopus can break off an arm if being attacked and can regrow it.

The SUCKERS are very sensitive. They are used for touching and tasting objects.

Glossary

invertebrate—a creature without a backbone

mantle—the sack-like body found behind the eyes of an octopus

mollusk—a soft-bodied creature that usually has a shell

oxygen—a gas in air that is important to all plants and animals

siphon—a tube-like organ found in mollusks, such as octopuses, that pushes water out of the body

venom—a poison that comes from the bite of an animal, such as an octopus or snake

Fun Facts

Smallest and Biggest
The smallest octopus is the Californian octopus. It is no longer than your thumbnail and weighs less than 1 once (28 grams). But the largest octopus, the North Pacific giant octopus, can be 28 feet (8.54 meters) long from arm tip to opposite arm tip. It can weigh 400 pounds (180 kilograms).

Protecting the Babies
While her eggs are developing, a mother octopus doesn't eat. She will leave her den only to protect her babies from other animals. After the octopuses are born, the mother usually dies of starvation.

Deadly Venom
Most octopus' venom isn't deadly to humans. But the blue-ringed octopus' venom is deadly. A blue-ringed octopus' bite has enough poison to stop a human's heart and breathing within two minutes.

Smarter Than You Might Think
Octopuses are smart. In scientific tests, they have learned to take the cork out of a bottle in order to get the food inside.

A Loner
An octopus likes to spend its time alone. But it will build its home near other octopuses of its size in order to mate.

Octopus Ice Cream?
Each year, fishermen catch from 20,000 to 100,000 tons (18,000 to 90,000 metric tons) of octopuses. Octopus is a popular food all over the world. In Japan, you can buy octopus-flavored ice cream!

Short Life Span
A common octopus lives for one to two years. Other kinds of octopuses can live up to three years.

To Learn More

More Books to Read

Kalman, Bobbie and Rebecca Sjonger. *The Amazing Octopus.* New York: Crabtree Pub., 2003.

Pitcher, Caroline. *Nico's Octopus.* New York: Crocodile Books, 2003.

Rhodes, Mary Jo and David Hall. *Octopuses and Squids.* New York: Children's Press, 2005.

Stone, Lynn. *Octopus.* Vero Beach, Fla.: Rourke Pub., 2006.

On the Web

FactHound offers a safe, fun way to find Web sites related to topics in this book. All of the sites on FactHound have been researched by our staff.

1. Visit www.facthound.com
2. Type in this special code: 1404847294
3. Click the FETCH IT button.

Your trusty FactHound will fetch the best sites for you!

Index

Look for all of the books in the I Live in the Ocean series:

I Am a Dolphin:
The Life of a Bottlenose Dolphin

I Am a Fish:
The Life of a Clown Fish

I Am a Sea Horse:
The Life of a Dwarf Sea Horse

I Am a Sea Turtle:
The Life of a Green Sea Turtle

I Am a Seal:
The Life of an Elephant Seal

I Am a Shark:
The Life of a Hammerhead Shark

I Am a Whale:
The Life of a Humpback Whale

I Am an Octopus:
The Life of a Common Octopus

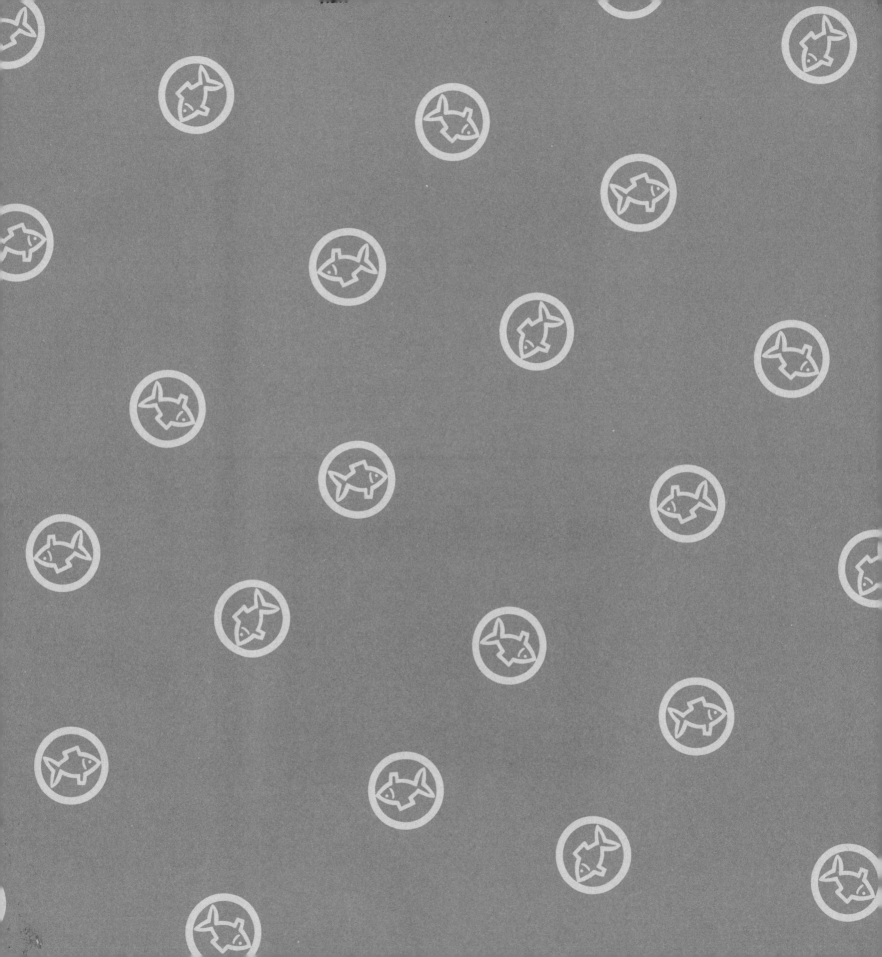